Community Helpers

Custodians

by Erika S. Manley

Bullfrog Books

Ideas for Parents and Teachers

Bullfrog Books let children practice reading informational text at the earliest reading levels. Repetition, familiar words, and photo labels support early readers.

Before Reading

- Discuss the cover photo. What does it tell them?
- Look at the picture glossary together. Read and discuss the words.

Read the Book

- "Walk" through the book and look at the photos. Let the child ask questions. Point out the photo labels.
- Read the book to the child, or have him or her read independently.

After Reading

- Prompt the child to think more. Ask: Do you know anyone who works as a custodian? Where does he or she work? What kinds of things does he or she do?

Bullfrog Books are published by Jump!
5357 Penn Avenue South
Minneapolis, MN 55419
www.jumplibrary.com

Copyright © 2018 Jump! International copyright reserved in all countries. No part of this book may be reproduced in any form without written permission from the publisher.

Library of Congress Cataloging-in-Publication Data

Names: Manley, Erika S., author.
Title: Custodians / by Erika S. Manley.
Description: Minneapolis, MN: Jump!, Inc., [2018]
Series: Community helpers Includes bibliographical references and index. | Audience: Age 5–8.
Audience: Grade K to grade 3.
Identifiers: LCCN 2016048139 (print)
LCCN 2016050329 (ebook)
ISBN 9781620316733 (hardcover: alk. paper)
ISBN 9781620317266 (pbk.)
ISBN 9781624965500 (ebook)
Subjects: LCSH: Janitors—Juvenile literature.
Buildings—Cleaning—Juvenile literature.
Industrial housekeeping—Juvenile literature.
Classification: LCC TX958 .M256 2018 (print)
LCC TX958 (ebook) | DDC 648/.5—dc23
LC record available at https://lccn.loc.gov/2016048139

Editor: Jenny Fretland VanVoorst
Book Designer: Leah Sanders
Photo Researcher: Leah Sanders

Photo Credits: Africa Studio/Shutterstock, cover; kurhan/Shutterstock, 1, 5; Seregam/Shutterstock, 3; Cultura Limited/SuperStock, 4; AndreyPopov/Shutterstock, 6; AndreyPopov/iStock, 7; Jim West/age fotostock/SuperStock, 8–9; Andrew Ushakov/Shutterstock, 10–11; Wstockstudio/Shutterstock, 10–11; Justin Geoffrey/Getty, 12–13; Katarzyna Bialasiewics/Dreamstime, 14–15; Photodiem/Shutterstock, 16–17; EHStock/Thinkstock, 18; AndreyPopov/Thinkstock, 19; fuse/Getty, 20–21; wabeno/iStock, 22; ND700/Shutterstock, 23tl; Andrewy Burmakin/Shutterstock, 23br; studiovin/Shutterstock, 24.

Printed in the United States of America at Corporate Graphics in North Mankato, Minnesota.

Table of Contents

Clean and Safe

Mattias wants to be a custodian.

What do they do?

They take care
of buildings.

They keep them
clean and safe.

They fix things that are broken.

Sue takes care
of a school.

Oh, no!

A child spilled milk.

Sue mops it up.

The floor is safe
to walk on again.

mop

The windows are dirty.
Sue washes them.
No more fingerprints!

Cho takes care
of an office.

She empties
the trash.

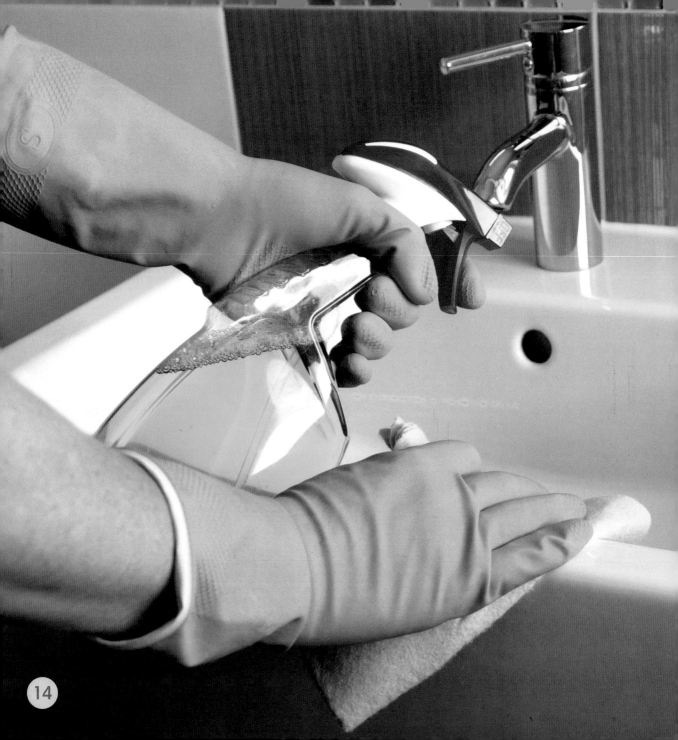

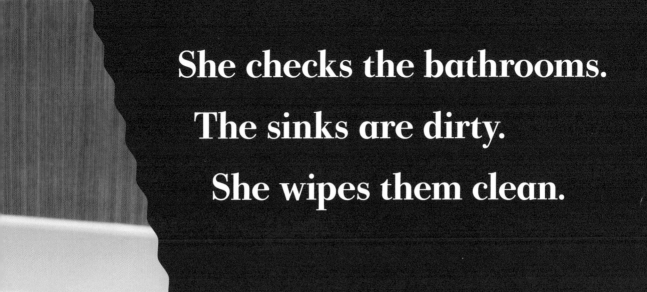

She checks the bathrooms.

The sinks are dirty.

She wipes them clean.

Nic takes care of an apartment building.

Oh, no!

The lights are out in the hall.

He changes the bulbs.

bulb

Nic gets a call.

Jen's oven won't work!

Nic comes to Jen's apartment.

He fixes the oven.

Yay! Now Jen can bake a cake!

Custodians do good work!

A Custodian's Tools

broom
A brush that has a long handle and is used for sweeping.

liquid cleaners
Liquids that are applied to hard surfaces in order to remove soil and germs.

vacuum cleaner
A device that uses suction to clean soft surfaces such as carpets.

mop
A tool for cleaning made of a bundle of cloth, yarn, or a sponge fastened to a handle.

Picture Glossary

apartment
A set of rooms used as a home, usually part of a building with many apartments.

custodian
A person who guards and protects or takes care of something.

broken
Having lost the ability to function because of damage, wear, or strain.

fingerprints
Marks made by pressing the tip of a finger on a surface.

Index

To Learn More

Learning more is as easy as 1, 2, 3.

1) Go to www.factsurfer.com

2) Enter "custodians" into the search box.

3) Click the "Surf" button to see a list of websites.

With factsurfer.com, finding more information is just a click away.